PILGRIM'S PROGRESS WORKBOOK for Kids

PILGRIM'S PROGRESS WORKBOOK for Kids

A Study Guide for *Pilgrim's Progress in Today's English*

Volume 2: Christiana's Journey

Caroline Weerstra

Catechism for Kids

Visit our website
www.catechismforkids.com

Published by Common Life Press, Schenectady, New York. 2012.

ISBN-13: 978-0983724988

This workbook is intended to accompany *Pilgrim's Progress in Today's English* by John Bunyan and James H. Thomas. All chapter titles, page numbers, characters, and other references to *Pilgrim's Progress in Today's English* are used by permission of Moody Publishers.

Except where otherwise noted, all Bible verses quoted in this workbook are in the New International (NIV) translation.

This workbook is a study guide intended to accompany the reading of

Pilgrim's Progress in Today's English

Authors: John Bunyan and James H. Thomas
Publisher: Moody Publishers

Contents

Introduction

John Bunyan's classic allegory was first published in February 1678 under the title *The Pilgrim's Progress from This Word to That Which Is to Come*. Written during a lengthy imprisonment by a man with little formal education, it nevertheless burst forth as an astounding success. It has become one of the most commonly read books of all time, and more than 300 years later, it has never been out of print.

John Bunyan's deep faith in Christ even amid great trials and suffering has inspired many generations after him. The storybook form in which he presents great theological concepts grasps the imagination of children and adults alike.

In *Pilgrim's Progress in Today's English*, James H. Thomas faithfully retells Bunyan's brilliant allegory in modern language. This is especially helpful for children, who love the story and characters of *Pilgrim's Progress* but may be discouraged by antiquated words and phrasing.

This workbook is intended as a children's study guide to accompany the reading of *Pilgrim's Progress in Today's English*. It encourages children to go beyond a simple enjoyment of the story and to think more deeply about the theological concepts underlying the characters and plot.

Each section of this workbook contains discussion of the meaning of the names of characters and the symbolism of various aspects of the story. Bible reading portions remind the readers of links between the allegory and the tenets of the Christian faith as found in Scripture. Finally, the application questions help students consider Scriptural principles in terms of real-life situations.

Pilgrim's Progress remains as relevant today as the day it was penned from the inside of a prison. The human condition persists in its error and folly, and so we catch glimpses of ourselves and those around us in the characters met by Christian and his companions on the road the Celestial City. Yet Pilgrim's Progress reminds us always of God's great faithfulness throughout generations, and we are encouraged to keep our eyes on Him as we travel the road of life.

Caroline Weerstra
January 6, 2012

CHAPTER 12: CHRISTIANA FOLLOWS CHRISTIAN

PART 1: A STRANGE VISITOR BRINGS A LETTER
READ PAGES 159–162.

BACKGROUND

John Bunyan's famous tale, *Pilgrim's Progress*, is divided into two main parts. The first part tells the story of Christian, and the second part tells the story of Christian's wife Christiana and her friend Mercy.

The first part of *Pilgrim's Progress* was published in 1678. Part 2 followed in 1684. For many years, these were published as separate books until they were combined in a single volume in 1728, long after John Bunyan had died.

It is known that Bunyan composed his books while he was imprisoned for preaching the gospel. Bunyan served two prison sentences. His first imprisonment

lasted for twelve years (1660 to 1672) with only a few weeks of freedom in 1666. His second imprisonment was much shorter—six months in 1675. Many scholars believe that he began his work on *Pilgrim's Progress* during his first stay in prison and finished it during his second.

John Bunyan's popularity as an author prevented him from being arrested again, and he was allowed comparative freedom for his later years. Despite the danger, he continued to preach for the rest of his life.

CHARACTERS

What do these characters' names mean?

Christiana: _____

Secret: _____

Mercy: _____

Answer the questions below:

1. In Part 1 of *Pilgrim's Progress*, Christian tried to persuade his wife to join him on his journey. How did she respond?

   _____

   _____

2. Who brought Christiana an invitation? _____

3. How did Christiana respond to the invitation? _____

   _____

4. Who joined Christiana on her journey?_____

5. Why did Mercy weep? _____

 ## SYMBOLISM

After Christian's death, Christiana begins to reflect on her harsh attitude toward him. She finally realizes that she is a sinner and that she needs salvation.

As she considers this, a messenger arrives with an invitation especially for her. She is invited to go to the Celestial City, just as Christian did. Christiana rejoices that God is ready to forgive her for rejecting the first offer. She sets out with her children and her friend Mercy.

As they travel toward the wicket gate, Mercy (who, as her name suggests, has a tender heart) weeps for those left behind. Christiana reminds her that Christian once wept for her, and now she has repented, and so perhaps in time, others who initially refuse to hear God's Word will repent.

John Bunyan begins the second part of *Pilgrim's Progress* with an encouraging reminder that God calls many people over time. Sometimes it may seem hopeless to imagine that a person will ever change, but God can soften hearts in many ways.

Christian did not live to see Christiana's change of heart, but his efforts still bore fruit in time. After he died, she remembered his words. Like Christian, we should never be discouraged about sharing the gospel. Even though we may never see the effect of our efforts during our lifetime, God may still use it in time to bring someone to repentance and faith in Christ.

BIBLE READING

Christiana comforted Mercy by reminding her of a particular Bible passage. Let's read it now:

Those who sow with tears will reap with songs of joy. Those who go out weeping, carrying seed to sow, will return with songs of joy, carrying sheaves with them. (Psalm 126:5-6)

Sowing (planting) is hard work. A farmer must go out carrying a heavy bag full of seeds to scatter. At first, it may seem as though nothing is happening. When the seeds are planted, the field still looks bare. However, under the ground, the seeds begin to sprout. In time, they grow and produce good food.

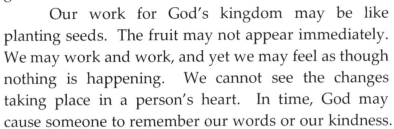

Our work for God's kingdom may be like planting seeds. The fruit may not appear immediately. We may work and work, and yet we may feel as though nothing is happening. We cannot see the changes taking place in a person's heart. In time, God may cause someone to remember our words or our kindness. Eventually, He may call them to repentance.

CONCLUSION

Read Galatians 6:9 in your Bible. Copy it here:

_____

_____

 REMEMBER! Never give up on sharing the gospel with others.

PART 2: AT THE GATE OF HOPE
READ PAGES 163-168.

DO YOU REMEMBER?

Christiana was sorry that she had been harsh to _____.

While she was thinking about this, a visitor named _____ arrived

with an _____ to the Celestial City.

Christiana set out on the journey with her _____ and her

friend _____. Mercy wept to think of those people left behind,

but _____ reminded her that others may follow later.

CHARACTERS

What does this character's name mean?

Keeper: _____

Answer the questions below:

1. What frightened Mercy and Christiana when they knocked at the gate?

   _____

2. Why did Mercy faint? _____

3. What did the Keeper show Mercy and Christiana from the top of the gatehouse?

   _____

4. Was the Keeper angry with Mercy for pounding on the gate?_____

5. Who owned the dangerous dog? _____

6. What happened when Christiana's sons ate the stolen fruit?

   _____

 SYMBOLISM

   Christiana has good confidence that she will be accepted by God. Until his death, her husband Christian had served God devoutly, and he had pleaded with her many times to join him on the journey. Mercy, on the other hand, feels as though she has no right to be a pilgrim. She has no special connection to Christian life. Mercy worries that perhaps God will reject her.

Ultimately, the determination of both Christiana and Mercy enables them to pass through the gate. They persist in knocking, even when they are frightened by the dog. When Mercy is left outside, she pounds on the gate frantically until Keeper lets her in.

God rewards those who seek Him. He wants us to be diligent in our Christian life. He provides us with the things we need to find the right path, but He wants us to use the things which He provides.

We are given God's Word, but we must read it. We are able to speak to God in prayer, but we must pray. God has established the church to help us, but we must attend and listen to the preaching. We must be active participants in faith, not lazy or timid.

Even though the pilgrims are on the right path, they are still faced with temptation. Christiana's sons eat the fruit which they see hanging over the wall. It is a dangerous mistake. They become seriously ill. Giving in to temptation is never healthy. Sin may appear harmless, but in time, we always discover that it is dangerous.

BIBLE READING

The book of Proverbs tells us to be diligent in seeking God:

> My son, if you accept my words and store up my commands within you, turning your ear to wisdom and applying your heart to understanding—indeed, if you call out for insight and cry aloud for understanding, and if you look for it as for silver and search for it as for hidden treasure, then you will understand the fear of the LORD and find the knowledge of God. For the LORD gives wisdom; from his mouth come knowledge and understanding. (Proverbs 2:1-6)

Wisdom comes from God, but we are commanded to search for it. The book of Proverbs instructs us to accept God's Word and to apply our hearts to understanding. Only then will we find the knowledge of God.

CONCLUSION

Suppose someone tells you, "I am a Christian. I once prayed and asked God to forgive my sins. I will go to heaven now, so I do not need to bother with praying anymore or reading my Bible or going to church."

How would you respond? _____

_____

 REMEMBER! God provides everything we need for Christian faith and life, but we must use the things God provides. We must seek Him diligently.

PART 3: DELIVERANCE FROM ATTACK
READ PAGES 168–169

DO YOU REMEMBER?

When Christiana and _____ knocked at the gate, they

were frightened by the barking of a _____. Christiana was let into

the gate by the _____ . However, _____ was

left outside. Mercy knocked frantically on the gate, and the _____

opened the _____ to let her in.

The Keeper showed Mercy and Christiana the _____ on the hill,

and he sent them on their way. Christiana's _____ ate some fruit

which was hanging over the wall. It made them _____ .

CHARACTERS

What does this character's name mean?

Reliever: _____

Answer the questions below:

1. What happened to Mercy and Christiana as they traveled down the path?

   _____

2. Who came to rescue them? _____

3. Reliever told the women they should have asked the Keeper for something. What was it?

   _____

4. How did Christiana believe this experience helped them?

   _____

   _____

   _____

SYMBOLISM

When Reliever rescues Christiana and Mercy, he chides them for their failure to ask for a guide. Christiana wonders why the Keeper does not provide guides without being asked, since he knows about the danger. Reliever tells her that if she were given everything she needs without asking, she would never know how dependent she is upon God's provision.

In this section, John Bunyan explains why God tells us to pray for the things we need. Sometimes people ask, "If God already knows what I need, why do I have to ask Him?"

John Bunyan explains that we realize our dependence on God when we are faced with difficult situations. If God simply gave us everything without being asked, then we would never know our own weakness. We would never understand how much we rely on His strength.

In the story, God delivers Christiana and Mercy in their distress, and He delivers us as well. However, we should never neglect to pray, and we should always remember that we are completely dependent upon His grace.

BIBLE READING

Jesus taught His disciples how to pray:

> And when you pray, you shall not be like the hypocrites. For they love to pray standing in the synagogues and on the corners of the streets, that they may be seen by men. Assuredly, I say to you, they have their reward. But you, when you pray, go into your room, and when you have shut your door, pray to your Father who is in the secret place; and your Father who sees in secret will reward you openly. And when you pray, do not use vain repetitions as the heathen do. For they think that they will be heard for their many words.

Therefore do not be like them. For your Father knows the things you have need of before you ask Him. In this manner, therefore, pray:

Our Father in heaven,
Hallowed be Your name.
Your kingdom come.
Your will be done
On earth as it is in heaven.
Give us this day our daily bread.
And forgive us our debts,
As we forgive our debtors.
And do not lead us into temptation,
But deliver us from the evil one.
For Yours is the kingdom and the power and the glory forever. Amen.

(Matthew 6:5-13 NKJV)

Jesus instructed His disciples to avoid praying like hypocrites, who pray only so that other people will be impressed. He also told them to have faith in God. The pagans think that praying for something over and over will make it more likely that God will hear them. God knows what we need before we even ask.

CONCLUSION

Jesus told His disciples to pray for daily bread. He meant that they should pray for everything they needed to live each day.

We are the disciples of Jesus today, and He wants us to pray for our daily bread also.

Does God know what we need before we ask? _____

Why should we pray for our daily bread when God knows what we need? (If you are not sure, think about Reliever's explanation to Christiana about the reason she should have asked for a guide.)

_____

_____

 REMEMBER! God knows everything we need, but He tells us to ask Him in prayer for all things, including our daily bread.

CHAPTER 13: AT THE INTERPRETER'S HOUSE

PART 1: OBJECT LESSONS SEEN (I)
READ PAGES 170-173.

DO YOU REMEMBER?

As Christiana, _____, and the children traveled along

the path, they were _____ by two men. A man named

_____ came to their rescue. He told Christiana that she

should have asked the Keeper for a _____ to help her on her way.

CHARACTERS

What do these characters' names mean?

Innocent: _____

Interpreter: _____

Answer the questions below:

1. How did Christiana and Mercy recognize the Interpreter's House?

    _____

2. Who met them at the door? _____

3. Why was the man with the muckrake unable to see the crown offered to him?

    _____

4. What did Mercy and Christiana find inside the finest room of the Interpreter's House?

    _____

5. What did the little chick do when it went to the trough to drink?

    _____

 SYMBOLISM

The Interpreter's House represents the process in which a new believer begins to understand truths about God. Christiana and Mercy have just started on their new path, but, with the help of the Interpreter, they quickly learn important concepts about God and Christian life.

The Interpreter teaches Christiana and Mercy the same lessons he taught Christian, but he adds a few more. He shows them a man with a muckrake. The man is so busy raking up muck that he never notices the crown held out to him. This symbolizes the tendency for many people to focus so much on gaining worldly things that they never pay attention to eternal matters. Worldly possessions are worthless compared to heavenly rewards, but nevertheless, many people prefer to rake the muck of the world instead of accepting the priceless treasure offered to them by God.

The second lesson arrives in the form of a spider hidden away in the finest room of the house. When Christiana and Mercy first search the room, they fail to even notice the spider. Only when they look carefully do they discover it. The spider represents sin which may hide away in the heart. Sin can be subtle and well-concealed. We must be careful to repent and confess our sin to God so that we do not hide a poisonous thing in our hearts.

Next, Christiana and Mercy observe two things about chickens. First, a little chick drinking from a trough demonstrates that we should all be thankful to God for His provision every day. Then, hearing the way the hen clucks—sometimes comforting, sometimes in warning—they understand that God also speaks to us in various ways. Sometimes God comforts us, and sometimes He warns us. Both of these reveal His love for us, like a hen loves and cares for her little chicks.

BIBLE READING

The apostle Paul reminds us to turn our hearts toward Christ rather than earthly things:

Since, then, you have been raised with Christ, set your hearts on things above, where Christ is, seated at the right hand of God. Set your minds on things above, not on earthly things. (Colossians 3:1-2)

We must remember that Christ is the center of all things in our lives. We work, play, go to school, and visit with our friends, but we should never be so caught up in those things that we forget God.

The main purpose of our lives is to glorify God and to enjoy Him forever. We should do everything with this purpose in mind. Our old sinful self has been buried with Christ, and we are raised to a new life in Him. We should live as people who have been redeemed.

CONCLUSION

Paul tells us to set our hearts on things above, not on earthly things. Think about how you can do this every day.

When you are at school, how can you show that your heart is set on things above?

_____

When you are doing your chores, how can you show that your heart is set on things above?

_____

When you are at church, how can you show that your heart is set on things above?

_____

 REMEMBER! Always remember Christ in everything you do!

PART 2: OBJECT LESSONS SEEN (II)
READ PAGES 174–175.

DO YOU REMEMBER?

Mercy, Christiana, and her sons arrived at the _____'s

House. They were welcomed, and the _____ showed them

many things. Among these was a man with a _____

who could not see the _____ offer to him. They also found

a _____ in a nice room, and they heard the way a _____

calls to the _____ .

Answer the questions below:

1. How did the sheep react toward the men who were hurting him?

   _____

2. What grew in the garden? _____

3. After the Interpreter had harvested the grain from his wheat field, what was left?

_____

4. What did Christiana suggest should be done with the straw?

_____

5. What was the robin eating? _____

 ## SYMBOLISM

The killing of the patient sheep is a symbol reminding us that we will suffer in our lives. We must bear the suffering quietly and patiently, just as Jesus did when He died on the cross. We should not complain or become bitter about difficulties. Rather, we should trust in God to help us endure.

The flower garden represents God's church. The church is full of all kinds of people—men, women, boys, and girls. They are old, young, rich, poor, tall, and short. Some of them are preachers, some are doctors, some are schoolteachers, some are soldiers, and so on. All of these people are important to God. Like flowers in a garden, they should live and work together, without boasting or quarrelling.

The wheat which has been harvested so that only straw is left in the field reminds us that fruit is important. If someone claims to love God but never obeys Him, then this person is like a plant with no fruit—it is no good at all.

The robin eating the spider symbolizes a Christian enjoying secret sin. The robin is beautiful bird, but it eats disgusting insects. Sometimes a person may pretend to love God while hiding secret sins. The Interpreter warns Christiana and Mercy to be honest and sincere in their faith.

BIBLE READING

In our story, the Interpreter compared the church to a flower garden. A garden may have many different kinds of flowers, but they all live together without complaining.

In the Bible, the apostle Paul compared the church to a body. The body is made up of many parts (eyes, ears, legs, hands, feet, and so on), but all the parts work together to make one body. Paul imagined what would happen if one body part began to complain or fight with other parts:

Just as a body, though one, has many parts, but all its many parts form one body, so it is with Christ. For we were all baptized by one Spirit so as to form one body—whether Jews or Gentiles, slave or free—and we were all given the one Spirit to drink. Even so the body is not made up of one part but of many. Now if the foot should say, "Because I am not a hand, I do not belong to the body," it would not for that reason stop being part of the body. And if the ear should say, "Because I am not an eye, I do not belong to the body," it would not for that reason stop being part of the body. If the whole body were an eye, where would the sense of hearing be? If the whole body were an ear, where would the sense of smell be? But in fact God has placed the parts in the body, every one of them, just as he wanted them to be. If they were all one part, where would the body be? As it is, there are many parts, but one body.

The eye cannot say to the hand, "I don't need you!" And the head cannot say to the feet, "I don't need you!" On the contrary, those parts of the body that seem to be weaker are indispensable, and the parts that we think are less

honorable we treat with special honor. And the parts that are unpresentable are treated with special modesty, while our presentable parts need no special treatment. But God has put the body together, giving greater honor to the parts that lacked it, so that there should be no division in the body, but that its parts should have equal concern for each other. If one part suffers, every part suffers with it; if one part is honored, every part rejoices with it. Now you are the body of Christ, and each one of you is a part of it.
(I Corinthians 12:12-27)

Paul reminded the Corinthians that a body cannot function without all of its parts. Some parts may seem more important than others, but each part is necessary. With this illustration, Paul showed us that each person is important. Each person has a particular role to fill, and so everyone must be content with what God has given them.

CONCLUSION

Suppose someone says, "I am not a pastor, so I am not anyone important. I don't matter to God at all."

How would you respond? _____

_____

Suppose someone says, "I am the church librarian, so I am very important. I am in charge of all the books! I am much more important than the Sunday School teachers!"

How would you respond? _____

_____

REMEMBER! In God's church, each person has an important role. We all need each other.

PART 3: PROVERBS HEARD AND
TESTIMONIES GIVEN
READ PAGES 175–178.

DO YOU REMEMBER?

The _____ showed his visitors the garden where

_____ grew all together without quarrelling. He also showed

them his _____ field where grain had been harvested. Only the

_____ remained, which was worthless. In the last lesson, they

observed a _____ with a _____ in its beak, which

represented the professing Christians secretly enjoying _____ .

Finish each proverb.

1. The fatter the sow…

_____

2. One leak will sink a ship, and...

_____

3. He who lives in sin and looks for happiness is like...

_____

_____

4. We seldom dine without leaving something on the table, so...

_____

_____

 SYMBOLISM

A **proverb** is a short saying which expresses a basic common-sense truth. The Interpreter uses proverbs to help his guests learn concepts about God and Christian life. He especially warns them that they must take sin seriously. He tells them that a sin is like a leak in a ship—it may seem small, but it will have serious consequences. He also explains that it is impossible to be happy as a sinner. At the moment of temptation, someone may think that sin will bring happiness, but in the end, it is like planting weeds in your garden—you get nothing for all your effort.

However, the Interpreter also assures Christiana and Mercy that Christ will always be enough for them. We are sinners, but Christ's righteousness is sufficient for us. When we put our faith in Christ, we receive forgiveness for our sins, and His righteousness is imputed to us.

Mercy has worried all throughout the journey that she does not have a proper invitation from God to be on the path. She thinks that she may be rejected. Sometimes we also may wonder if God has truly chosen us or whether He has chosen someone else who may be smarter or more talented or have other qualities useful for His kingdom. In the story, Mercy is not turned away, and neither is anyone else who comes to God. He accepts all who come to Him in faith and repentance.

BIBLE READING

The Interpreter comforted Mercy by comparing her to Ruth in the Bible. Ruth was not born among God's people. She was born in a country called Moab, and she most likely grew up worshiping false gods.

Ruth's life changed when she met Naomi. Naomi was an Israelite woman who knew the true God. She had moved to Moab with her husband Elimelek and her two sons Mahlon and Kilion. They went to Moab because of a famine in Israel. Naomi and her family stayed in Moab for a long time. Naomi's two sons married Moabite women: Orpah and Ruth. Then Naomi's husband died.

The Bible tells the story:

After they had lived there about ten years, both Mahlon and Kilion also died, and Naomi was left without her two sons and her husband.

When Naomi heard in Moab that the LORD had come to the aid of his people by providing food for them, she and her daughters-in-law prepared to return home from there. With her two daughters-in-law she left the place where she had been living and set out on the road that would take them back to the land of Judah.

Then Naomi said to her two daughters-in-law, "Go back, each of you, to your mother's home. May the LORD show you kindness, as you have shown kindness to your dead husbands and to me. May the LORD grant that each of you will find rest in the home of another husband."

Then she kissed them goodbye and they wept aloud and said to her, "We will go back with you to your people."

But Naomi said, "Return home, my daughters. Why would you come with me? Am I going to have any more sons, who could become your husbands? Return home, my daughters; I am too old to have another husband. Even if I thought there was still hope for me—even if I had a husband tonight and then gave birth to sons—would you wait until they grew up? Would you remain unmarried for them? No, my daughters. It is more bitter for me than for you, because the LORD's hand has turned against me!"

At this they wept aloud again. Then Orpah kissed her mother-in-law goodbye, but Ruth clung to her.

"Look," said Naomi, "your sister-in-law is going back to her people and her gods. Go back with her."

But Ruth replied, "Don't urge me to leave you or to turn back from you. Where you go I will go, and where you stay I will stay. Your people will be my people and your God my God. Where you die I will die, and there I will be buried. May the LORD deal with me, be it ever so severely, if even death separates you and me." When Naomi realized that Ruth was determined to go with her, she stopped urging her. (Ruth 1:4-18)

As a Moabite woman, Ruth did not have the same claim to the covenant that Naomi did. However, she was determined to stay with Naomi and to worship the true God. Her persistence revealed that she was indeed one of God's chosen people. God blessed Ruth and gave her every benefit of the covenant. In fact, Ruth was the great-grandmother of King David, the greatest king in Israelite history.

CONCLUSION

Christiana and Mercy told their **testimonies** (their stories about how they became followers of Christ) to the Interpreter. The Bible tells the testimony of Ruth and many others.

What is your testimony? Did you hear about Jesus from your parents? Or perhaps from a friend? Or at Vacation Bible School? Describe how you first learned about God.

_____

_____

_____

_____

 REMEMBER! God never turns people away who come to Him in faith and repentance.

CHAPTER 14: THE GUIDANCE OF GREATHEART

PART 1: THE CROSS
READ PAGES 179–182.

DO YOU REMEMBER?

The Interpreter taught his guests some _____ . Then

Christiana and _____ told how they had become pilgrims. The

Interpreter said that Mercy was like _____ in the Bible. This made

Mercy very _____.

CHARACTERS

What do these characters' names mean?

Greatheart: _____

Slowpace: _____

Shortwind: _____

Noheart: _____

Lingerlust: _____

Mr. Sleepy: _____

Dull: _____

Answer the questions below:

1. Who traveled with Christiana, Mercy, and the children to guide them?

    _____

2. While they were looking at the cross, what did Christiana worry that she did not understand?

    _____

    _____

3. When Christiana wondered how Christ could have enough righteousness left for Himself, what did Greatheart say?

_____

_____

4. According to Greatheart, does everyone love Jesus?

_____

5. Why had Simple, Sloth, and Presumption been hanged?

_____

_____

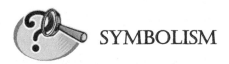 SYMBOLISM

When the pilgrims reach the cross, Christiana confides to her guide that she does not yet fully understand salvation. Greatheart explains the concept which John Bunyan refers to as 'pardon by deed.' You may have heard of this before (perhaps in church) described as **atonement**. Jesus lived a perfect, sinless life. His righteousness is given to us so that we are made righteous. He died to **atone** for our sins. This means that the sacrifice of His body and blood on the cross paid for our sins. He took the punishment for our sins on Himself. Because of Christ's atonement, we are no longer under God's judgment.

When Christiana and Mercy understand the atonement of Christ, they are very grateful to God. We also should be thankful for the forgiveness of sins which Christ purchased through His blood. We should remember His sacrifice for us, and our thankfulness should propel us toward obedience to His Word.

Greatheart warns, however, that not everyone responds as they should. Even some of the people who saw Jesus die on the cross were ungrateful and unmerciful to Him. They mocked Him as He died.

John Bunyan continues this idea in the next section in which he discusses the three sleepers: Simple, Sloth, and Presumption. In the first part of *Pilgrim's Progress*, Christian discovered these three men as well. He tried to warn them about their danger, but they ignored him. It appears that after Christian's warning, these men became even worse. They stirred up trouble in the church. They made false accusations against other believers. They even blasphemed God and tried to discourage other people from following Him.

The hanging of these three men represents church discipline carried out against those people who reveal that they are not true believers. Sometimes the church has a duty to punish church members who do terrible things. The church does not literally hang people, but it may declare that certain people are no longer part of the church and that they cannot receive the Lord's Supper until they repent. Sometimes, wicked people do repent and turn back to God. They are received back into the church. If they refuse to repent, however, then they are outside the church of Christ. This serves as a warning to others.

John Bunyan often reminds his readers that God's warnings are for our good. God is patient for a while, even with people like Simple, Sloth, and Presumption who cause great trouble. These three men sat on the path sleeping for a long time, and many other pilgrims tried to wake them, but to no avail. When Simple, Sloth, and Presumption began hurting other people, however, something had to be done to stop them. The church has a duty to protect the souls in its care.

BIBLE READING

Jesus gave clear instructions to His disciples regarding how to deal with sin in the church:

> If your brother or sister sins, go and point out their fault, just between the two of you. If they listen to you, you have won them over. But if they will not listen, take one or two others along, so that 'every matter may be established by the testimony of two or three witnesses.' If they still refuse to listen, tell it to the church; and if they refuse to listen even to the church, treat them as you would a pagan or a tax collector. Truly I tell you, whatever you bind on earth will be bound in heaven, and whatever you loose on earth will be loosed in heaven. (Matthew 18:15-18)

Jesus commanded His disciples to have patience even with someone who has sinned against them. The first step in dealing with a serious sin is *not* to go around telling everyone. The first step is to speak to the person who has sinned alone, thereby giving the sinner a chance to repent without ruining his reputation in the community.

The second step (if he does not repent) is to bring along two or three others. Perhaps the sinner may scoff at just one person, but he may take the matter more seriously if several others warn him also.

Eventually, if the guilty person does not repent, then the matter must be brought before the whole church. If the sinner ignores the whole church, then he should be set outside the church and treated as if he were not a Christian at all.

Jesus warned that this judgment (if it is in accord with God's Word) is binding. A person who has been set outside the church is considered an unbeliever in heaven as well as on earth. Such a sinner should not comfort himself by imagining that he will go to heaven anyway.

However, this is not the end of the matter. Jesus also told His disciples, "If your brother or sister sins against you, rebuke them; and if they repent, forgive them." (Luke 17:3)

We are all sinners, and we all need to be rebuked sometimes. The question is whether we repent when we are rebuked. Simple, Sloth, and Presumption did not. Church discipline is not for people who repent. It is for those who refuse to repent even when they are warned. Forgiveness is always available for people who love God and repent of their sins. As Greatheart said, "Christ has more righteousness than He and all the world will ever need. Therefore, it is free to all who come by faith."

CONCLUSION

Think about this story and answer the questions:

Margaret attended a small church in Missouri. One Sunday morning, just before the worship service, Margaret took twenty dollars out of her purse. She was going to put it in the church offering basket. While she was talking to her friends, however, she set the money down on a table and forgot about it.

Margaret remembered the money and came back to get it. Just as she walked around the corner, she saw another church member, Carl, pick up the money from the table and put it into his pocket.

Margaret was shocked. She ran back to her friends and said, "Carl stole my twenty dollars!"

Did Margaret respond correctly?

_____

What should Margaret have done? _____

_____

It is possible that Carl stole the money, but it is also possible that he picked it up to take it to the lost-and-found box. This is one reason that it is so important to talk to someone before accusing that person in front of everyone.

Suppose Margaret talked to Carl, and he said, "You are right, Margaret. I did steal the money. I saw it sitting there, and thought it was lost. I thought no one would notice and it wouldn't matter. But I see now that I was wrong. I will pay your money back. Will you forgive me?"

What should Margaret do? _____

 REMEMBER! When people sin against you, talk to them before you tell everyone. If they repent, forgive them.

PART 2: THE HILL OF DIFFICULTY
AND THE GIANT
READ PAGES 182–187.

DO YOU REMEMBER?

The travelers arrived at the _____ . Christiana told

_____ that she did not quite understand salvation.

Greatheart explained _____ , and Christiana and Mercy

were amazed and happy. Later, they saw _____ , Sloth, and

_____ , who had been _____ for their

_____ deeds.

CHARACTERS

What does this character's name mean?

Grim: _____

Answer the questions below:

1. Was Christiana tempted to go around the Hill of Difficulty?

   _____

2. What did Greatheart do when Christiana's son James began to cry?

   _____

3. Why did Christiana forget the bottle of juice in the arbor?

   _____

4. Who killed the giant Grim? _____

 SYMBOLISM

Christiana is more confident in her faith than her husband Christian, and this is due in part to her recollections of his pilgrim journey. Christiana is not seriously tempted to try to go around the Hill of Difficulty. Greatheart reminds her of Christian's experience there with Formality and Hypocrisy, so Christiana is able to avoid trouble easily.

We may learn from the experiences of others to help us in our faith. The Bible has many stories about believers, including their temptations and mistakes. The Scriptures even tell us about some people who began to follow God but turned aside to destruction. We are warned of these things so that we can learn.

The Giant Grim is an interesting villain. He appears to believe that he has a right to be on the path. He declares that he is merely defending his own ground.

There are indeed many evil people who believe that they are doing right. They may oppose God because they think they know better than He does. This is evil, but their minds are twisted so that they believe they are acting for good.

Greatheart kills Grim with his sword. The sword represents the

Word of God. Only the Word of God is truly good. We find God's will in the Bible, not in our own thoughts. Even though Grim imagines that he is right, he becomes evil when he fights against the Word of God.

BIBLE READING

The Bible tells a story about a man named Saul who thought he was doing a good thing by fighting against God's people. Saul was so convinced that Christians were dangerous that he started gathering them up and putting them in prison. Let's read the story:

Meanwhile, Saul was still breathing out murderous threats against the Lord's disciples. He went to the high priest and asked him for letters to the synagogues in Damascus, so that if he found any there who belonged to the Way, whether men or women, he might take them as prisoners to Jerusalem.

As he neared Damascus on his journey, suddenly a light from heaven flashed around him. He fell to the ground and heard a voice say to him, "Saul, Saul, why do you persecute me?"

"Who are you, Lord?" Saul asked.

"I am Jesus, whom you are persecuting," he replied. "Now get up and go into the city, and you will be told what you must do."

The men traveling with Saul stood there speechless; they heard the sound but did not see anyone. Saul got up from the ground, but when he opened his eyes he could see nothing. So they led him by the hand into Damascus. For three days he was blind, and did not eat or drink anything.

In Damascus there was a disciple named Ananias. The Lord called to him in a vision, "Ananias!"

"Yes, Lord," he answered.

The Lord told him, "Go to the house of Judas on Straight Street and ask for a man from Tarsus named Saul, for he is praying. In a vision he has seen a man named Ananias come and place his hands on him to restore his sight."

"Lord," Ananias answered, "I have heard many reports about this man and all the harm he has done to your holy people in Jerusalem. And he has come here with authority from the chief priests to arrest all who call on your name."

But the Lord said to Ananias, "Go! This man is my chosen instrument to proclaim my name to the Gentiles and their kings and to the people of Israel. I will show him how much he must suffer for my name."

Then Ananias went to the house and entered it. Placing his hands on Saul, he said, "Brother Saul, the Lord—Jesus, who appeared to you on the road as you were coming here—has sent me so that you may see again and be filled with the Holy Spirit."

Immediately, something like scales fell from Saul's eyes, and he could see again. He got up and was baptized, and after taking some food, he regained his strength. Saul spent several days with the disciples in Damascus. (Acts 9:1-19)

When Jesus appeared to Saul and spoke to him, Saul realized that he was wrong to fight against God's people. Even though he had thought he was doing the right thing, he was really doing a very wicked thing. He repented, and God forgave him.

CONCLUSION

Saul later became known as **Paul**. He became an apostle and preached the gospel everywhere. He never forgot the words of Jesus, and he never again fought against God's people. In fact, we have read portions of Paul's letters to the churches in this book already. They are quotations from the Bible.

What are some of the letters Saul/Paul wrote? _____

_____

Which book of the Bible tells us about Saul/Paul's missionary journeys?

_____

 REMEMBER!   Righteousness is found only in obedience to the Word of God.

CHAPTER 15: AT THE PORTER'S LODGE

PART 1: THE CATECHISM
READ PAGES 188-195.

DO YOU REMEMBER?

The pilgrims arrived at the Hill of _____ . Christiana's

son _____ needed the help of _____ to climb

the hill. However, they managed to ascend to the _____ to rest.

When they came upon the chained _____ , a giant named

_____ appeared. He claimed that he was the owner of the grounds.

_____ killed the giant with his _____ .

CHARACTERS

What do these characters' names mean?

Humble: _____

Prudence: _____

Piety: _____

Charity: _____

Answer the questions below:

1. Where did Greatheart take Christiana, Mercy, and the children?

    _____

2. Where did Christiana and Mercy sleep? _____

    _____

3. What did Mercy dream? _____

    _____

    _____

4. Who asked the children questions about God? _____

5. What advice did Prudence give the children?

_____

_____

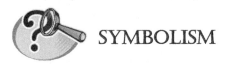 SYMBOLISM

Greatheart leaves the pilgrims at the Porter's Lodge. Perhaps because of her nervousness about being alone on her journey, Christiana asks if she may stay in the same room Christian stayed in. This symbolizes again her determination to learn from others, and especially her eagerness to remember everything Christian had told her about his journey.

Mercy stays in the same room, and she dreams about being welcomed into the Celestial City. Christiana and Mercy are both very encouraged by

this dream. They realize that they belong to God. No matter what troubles they may encounter on the journey, God will welcome them into heaven.

At times when we feel alone, we should remember that other believers have lived in faith before us. When we remember this, we know that God will help us just as He helped them. No matter what trouble may come upon us in life, God will not leave us.

Another good reminder of God's promises may be found in the catechism. The catechism is a summary of the teaching of Scripture, and it is often used to teach children about God. It is a series of questions which children learn to answer properly.

Prudence tests Christiana's children on the catechism. She is pleased to discover that they know it well. She advises them to continue to listen to their mother and to other older pilgrims.

The Bible tells us to respect our parents and those who have lived long in the faith. They may have wisdom from their experiences and studies, and we should be willing to learn.

BIBLE READING

Psalm 78 declares the importance of learning from our ancestors in the faith—our parents and all the faithful who have gone before us:

> My people, hear my teaching;
> listen to the words of my mouth.
> I will open my mouth with a parable;
> I will utter hidden things, things from of old—
> things we have heard and known,
> things our ancestors have told us.
> We will not hide them from their descendants;
> we will tell the next generation
> the praiseworthy deeds of the LORD,
> his power, and the wonders he has done.

> He decreed statutes for Jacob
> and established the law in Israel,
> which he commanded our ancestors
> to teach their children,
> so the next generation would know them,
> even the children yet to be born,
> and they in turn would tell their children.
> Then they would put their trust in God
> and would not forget his deeds
> but would keep his commands.
> (Psalm 78:1-7)

God commands each generation of His people to teach their children the Word of God.

CONCLUSION

Do you know your catechism? There are several catechisms, including the *Westminster Shorter Catechism* and the *Heidelberg Catechism*. For generations, parents have used these to teach their children about God.

Can you answer the questions? (If not, ask your parent or teacher to help you look up the answers):

Westminster Shorter Catechism, Question 1:

What is the chief end of man?

_____

_____

Heidelberg Catechism, Question 1:

What is your only comfort in life and death?

_____

_____

_____

 REMEMBER! Learn your catechism!

PART 2: MERCY'S SUITOR
READ PAGES 195–197.

DO YOU REMEMBER?

The guide _____ left Christiana, Mercy, and

the children at the _____'s Lodge. _____

and Mercy stayed in the room in which _____ had slept

during his stay at the Porter's Lodge. _____ had a dream

which encouraged her about the hope of _____.

Later, _____ questioned Christian's sons on their

_____. She was glad to find that they had learned it well.

CHARACTERS

What do these characters' names mean?

Mr. Brisk _____

Bountiful: _____

Answer the questions below:

1. Why did Mr. Brisk want to marry Mercy?

   _____

2. What was Mercy doing which caused Mr. Brisk to change his mind?

   _____

3. What happened to Mercy's sister Bountiful?

   _____

   _____

 SYMBOLISM

In the story of Mercy's suitor, John Bunyan warns his readers against marrying someone who is not a believer. He warns especially that Christians must be careful that the person they marry is a *true* believer, not just someone who claims to believe in God.

Life can be very hard for a Christian who marries a non-Christian. A non-Christian husband or wife may be set against going to church, teaching children about God, or even doing good works for others (as Mercy discovered with her suitor).

John Bunyan cautions his readers especially about hypocrites. Many believers have married someone who claimed to be a Christian but later turned out to care nothing about God. It is important to be sure of the sincerity of the faith of a prospective spouse *before* agreeing to marry. Mercy wisely declares that she would rather remain single than be joined in marriage to anyone who does not truly possess faith in Christ.

BIBLE READING

John Bunyan warned against marriage with unbelievers. The Bible warns us against this as well:

> Do not be yoked together with unbelievers. For what do righteousness and wickedness have in common? Or what fellowship can light have with darkness? What harmony is there between Christ and Belial? Or what does a believer have in common with an unbeliever? (II Corinthians 6:14-15)

A **yoke** is a farm tool. It is a piece of wood laid across the necks of two oxen to join them together so that they can plow a field at the same time (see the picture). Can you imagine what would happen if one ox wanted to plow and the other one refused? They would not go very far! Life would be difficult for the ox that wanted to plow if the other ox would not agree.

This Bible passage forbids us to be yoked with unbelievers (in marriage, for example). If one wants to follow Jesus and the other will not agree, life can be very hard for the Christian. It may be nearly impossible to serve Christ as they should.

When a Christian marries another Christian, then they both have a common goal—serving Jesus. They can work together and encourage each other in faith.

CONCLUSION

Suppose someone says, "It doesn't matter if I marry a non-Christian. I can still go to church and serve God!"

How would you respond to this? _____

_____

 REMEMBER! God's Word declares that we should not be yoked together with unbelievers.

PART 3: OBJECT LESSONS
READ PAGES 197–201.

DO YOU REMEMBER?

A man named Mr. _____ wanted to marry Mercy.

However, when he realized that she was helping the _____,

he changed his mind. Mercy spoke of her sister _____

who had _____ a man who claimed to be a Christian but

was not sincere in obedience to _____ .

CHARACTERS

What do these characters' names mean?

Prudence: _____

Piety: _____

Answer the questions below:

1. According to Prudence, what was the lesson to be learned from sparks and sunbeams?

    _____

    _____

2. What did Prudence say should be remembered when we hear a rooster crow?

    _____

    _____

3. What message did Christiana send to the Interpreter?

    _____

4. What was the significance of the fruit that the people at the Porter's House showed to the pilgrims?

    _____

5. What sang the song with the lyrics, "The Lord our God is good"?

    _____

 SYMBOLISM

At the Porter's House, Christiana and her companions learn lessons about God in everyday surroundings. They learn to recognize God's promises in rainbows, to think of God's mercy when they see sunbeams, and to hear even the birds singing the praises of God.

When we realize that God has made all things and that all things are for His glory, we begin to recognize God's handiwork all around us. The rainbows symbolize His faithfulness. The light and air are gifts from God. Everything around us can teach us lessons about God's love and care for His creatures.

BIBLE READING

King David wrote about the wonders of God's glory expressed in His creation:

> The heavens declare the glory of God;
> the skies proclaim the work of his hands.
> Day after day they pour forth speech;
> night after night they reveal knowledge.
> They have no speech, they use no words;
> no sound is heard from them.
> Yet their voice goes out into all the earth,
> their words to the ends of the world.
> (Psalm 19:1-4)

David sang that even the sky proclaims God's handiwork. Even though it does not speak, we can look at it and marvel at God's glory.

Nature is only a work of God. God is the Creator of everything. Yet we can see the glory of God expressed in all things He has made.

CONCLUSION

Is there something in God's creation that amazes you? Think of the wonders of God's universe—the planets, the stars, waterfalls, oceans, animals, trees, and flowers.

Draw a picture of something which reminds you of God's glory:

 REMEMBER! All creation demonstrates the glory of God, our Creator. We can look around us and see God's handiwork.

CHAPTER 16: WITH GREATHEART ON THE WAY

PART 1: THE VALLEYS
READ PAGES 202-208.

DO YOU REMEMBER?

_____ taught Matthew many lessons from nature

which served to illustrate truths about _____. Christiana

sent a message to the _____ asking that their guide

_____ be returned to them.

CHARACTERS

What do these characters' names mean?

Heedless: _____

Takeheed: _____

Answer the questions below:

1. According to Greatheart, why had Apollyon attacked Christian in the Valley of Humility?

   _____

2. Was everyone attacked in the Valley of Humility? _____

3. What song did the barefoot boy sing? _____

   _____

   _____

4. What happened when the pilgrims approached the imp of darkness?

   _____

   _____

5. Who was lying dead at the end of the Valley of the Shadow of Death?

   _____

 SYMBOLISM

The pilgrims find the Valley of Humility to be a peaceful, happy place. Greatheart assures them that it is a comfortable home for many people and that Jesus once lived there. The trouble in the valley always begins when someone is unable to adjust to humiliation.

This valley illustrates an important truth about Christian life. Many people live simple, happy lives if they are humble enough to accept their circumstances. When people are proud, they grumble and struggle against jealousy and discontent. They think too highly of themselves. They cannot adjust to being average people with no great power or influence. If Christians are humble, they have nothing to fear from being in humble circumstances. They are grateful for their work and their daily life, and they honor and serve God.

When we feel humbled, we should remember that Jesus lived a very humble life. Jesus is the eternal Son of God, and yet He was born on earth in a stable, and He grew up in Nazareth as the son of a carpenter. He died a terrible, shameful death on the cross for us. If Jesus was humble, then we should be humble also.

In the Valley of the Shadow of Death, the pilgrims discover that many dangers (such as the imp of darkness and the lion) are illusions. Christiana, Mercy, and the children may be frightened by something looming up ahead or sneaking up behind them, but when they faced it firmly, it disappears. Many things we face are also scarier in our minds than they are in reality. If we stand against them, we realize that God defends us. We have no need to fear.

The last lesson in the Valley of the Shadow of Death dwells on the importance of having other Christians around us, especially friends on whom we can rely to lead us in the right direction. Mr. Heedless died because he would not travel with a guide. He tried to go through Christian life on his own, and he could not.

 ## BIBLE READING

The verse quoted by Greatheart about humility is found in Peter's first epistle:

> In the same way, you who are younger, submit yourselves to your elders. All of you, clothe yourselves with humility toward one another, because, "God opposes the proud but shows favor to the humble." (I Peter 5:5)

This verse reminds us that we should listen to others and be guided by them, especially Christians who are older and wiser than ourselves. We should also be humble. Humility enables us to accept correction and guidance from wise people who instruct us about God's Word. God shows favor to those who are humble.

CONCLUSION

Look up Psalm 25: 8-9 in your Bible and copy it here:

_____

_____

_____

REMEMBER! God shows favor to the humble.

PART 2: GIANT MAUL
READ PAGES 208-210.

DO YOU REMEMBER?

The pilgrims, led by their guide _____, entered

the Valley of _____. They saw the place where Christian

had fought _____, but they were not attacked. For them,

it was a Valley of _____ .

Next, they went into the Valley of the Shadow of _____ .

They saw an _____ of darkness, but it _____ as

they approached it. At the end of the valley, they saw _____,

who had died because of traveling without a _____.

CHARACTERS

What does this character's name mean?

Maul _____

Answer the questions below:

1. Who came out of the cave of Pope and Pagan?

    _____

2. What did the giant accuse Greatheart of doing?

    _____

3. Where did the pilgrims sit down to rest?

    _____

 SYMBOLISM

Giant Maul symbolizes an attack of Satan against someone who shepherds God's people. The giant takes no interest in fighting the women and children. He wants to take them as prisoners by killing their guide. At first, he makes false accusations against Greatheart, and then he attacks him with force.

Satan often seeks to destroy believers by attacking those who lead them. Pastors, elders, and other church leaders have many challenges and many responsibilities. We should always pray for our leaders and encourage them as we are able.

BIBLE READING

God used the ministry of the apostle Paul to establish many churches. However, Paul was often attacked for his preaching. He was sometimes beaten. Eventually, he was placed in prison. From prison, he wrote letters to instruct and encourage the churches. He also asked that they would pray for him and for other church leaders:

And pray for us, too, that God may open a door for our message, so that we may proclaim the mystery of Christ, for which I am in chains. Pray that I may proclaim it clearly, as I should. (Colossians 4:3-4)

Even the great apostle Paul needed the prayers of the church, and our leaders also need our prayers.

CONCLUSION

Who are your leaders?

Who leads your family at home? _____

Who teaches you in school? _____

Who is your pastor? _____

Who are your elders? _____

 REMEMBER! Pray for your leaders.

```
┌─────────────────────────────────────────────┐
│            PART 3:  MR. HONESTY               │
│            READ PAGES 211–218.                │
└─────────────────────────────────────────────┘
```

DO YOU REMEMBER?

As the pilgrims approached the cave of _____ and Pagan,

a giant named _____ came out and attacked _____ .

Greatheart fought and finally _____ the giant.

The pilgrims set up a _____ and then sat to rest at

the place where Christian had first seen _____ .

CHARACTERS

What do these characters' names mean?

Mr. Honesty: _____

Mr. Fearing: _____

Mr. Selfwill: _____

Answer the questions below:

1. Whom did the pilgrims find sleeping under a tree?

    _____

2. From which city had Mr. Honesty traveled? _____

3. Why did Mr. Fearing take so long to knock at the wicket gate?

    _____

4. Was Mr. Fearing afraid of people in Vanity Fair? _____

5. Mr. Selfwill read about sins in the Bible, and then what did he think he could do?

    _____

 SYMBOLISM

In the stories told by Mr. Honesty, we learn of a man named Mr. Fearing. This man is a strange mixture of fear and courage. Sometimes he is incredibly timid, and other times he faces down enemies with great courage.

John Bunyan uses the character of Mr. Fearing to illustrate the idea that there are different types of fear. Some people are too afraid of the opinions of others. Some people tend to fear themselves and their own sinfulness. Mr. Fearing is not afraid of other people. He does not mind being humble at all. He is not afraid of the dangers of the City of Vanity. He fears his own sinfulness. In some ways, this is good—it helps him to avoid some of the traps other people fall into. However, it can also be bad. Mr. Fearing suffers needlessly because of his own timidity.

We see that God is very gracious to Mr. Fearing. Even the Valley of the Shadow of Death is quieter for him than for others. God preserves those who are humble and faithful, even when they are timid, silly creatures.

As a contrast to Mr. Fearing, Mr. Honesty tells about Selfwill, who wants to do whatever he likes, even if it is sinful. Selfwill ignores all the warnings in the Bible and uses anything he can find to excuse his sin. Selfwill is the complete opposite of Mr. Fearing. Mr. Fearing always shrinks back from sin, and sometimes he will even worry he has sinned when he has not. Selfwill is confident and bold, but in a very bad way.

Fear is not always bad, if it is fear of a proper thing. Confidence is not always good, if confidence is not founded upon God's Word. Ultimately, we are called to serve God.

BIBLE READING

In *Pilgrim's Progress*, we see an illustration of God's compassion in the kindness Mr. Fearing receives on his journey. Mr. Fearing is afraid of everything, and in some ways, his life is difficult. However, he ultimately overcomes all obstacles with the help of God and with the guidance of Greatheart.

God is merciful to His children. He knows that we are weak. He never tempts us with something bigger than we can manage. Psalm 103 talks about God's compassion:

> As a father has compassion on his children,
> so the LORD has compassion on those who fear him;
> for he knows how we are formed,
> he remembers that we are dust.
> The life of mortals is like grass,
> they flourish like a flower of the field;
> the wind blows over it and it is gone,
> and its place remembers it no more.
> But from everlasting to everlasting
> the LORD's love is with those who fear him,
> and his righteousness with their children's children—
> with those who keep his covenant
> and remember to obey his precepts.
>
> (Psalm 103:13-18)

CONCLUSION

According to Psalm 103, God has compassion because He remembers that we are made from dust. What does this mean?

_____

_____

 REMEMBER! God is merciful to His children. Even when we are weak, He loves us and provides for us.

CHAPTER 17: AT THE HOMES OF GAIUS AND MNASON

PART 1: THE HOME OF GAIUS
READ PAGES 219-222.

DO YOU REMEMBER?

The pilgrims found an old man sleeping under a _____.

When they woke him, he said his name was _____ and that

he had left the town of _____ . As they all walked on together,

Honesty talked about Mr. _____ who had a very difficult life.

He also mentioned Selfwill, who always thought up excuses to _____.

CHARACTERS

What does this character's name mean?

Slaygood: _____

Answer the questions below:

1. Where did Greatheart take the pilgrims to stay when they were tired?

    _____

2. Was Gaius kind to his guests? _____

3. What did Gaius ask the pilgrims to do? _____

    _____

4. Who was held captive by Slaygood? _____

 SYMBOLISM

Gaius is **hospitable** to pilgrims. This means that he welcomes them and treats them with kindness and generosity. The kindness of Gaius extends beyond those who are in his own house, however. He looks for ways to help everyone, including Mr. Weak. Gaius organizes a rescue team to kill the robber who is holding Mr. Weak captive.

There are many people held captive by the snares of Satan. Perhaps some are deceived by false teachings, fall into temptation, or other such things. The example of Gaius shows that it is a kindness to try to help others. We should not be cold to their difficulties. Some people may be weaker than us. They may fall into Satan's traps easily. We must try to protect them and rescue them when they are ensnared.

BIBLE READING

In the Bible, **Gaius** was a real person. He is mentioned in the book of Romans:

> Gaius, whose hospitality I and the whole church here enjoy, sends you his greetings. (Romans 16:23)

The Scriptures tell us many times that we should be hospitable toward others and care for the needs of people around us. Gaius did this very well. The whole church enjoyed his hospitality.

Jesus told a parable about God's concern for the way we care for others. He pictured Himself as a shepherd separating sheep from goats in His flock:

> "When the Son of Man comes in his glory, and all the angels with him, he will sit on his glorious throne. All the nations will be gathered before him, and he will separate the people one from another as a shepherd separates the sheep from the goats. He will put the sheep on his right and the goats on his left.
>
> "Then the King will say to those on his right, 'Come, you who are blessed by my Father; take your inheritance, the kingdom prepared for you since the creation of the world. For I was hungry and you gave me something to eat, I was thirsty and you gave me something to drink, I was a stranger and you invited me in, I needed clothes and you clothed me, I was sick and you looked after me, I was in prison and you came to visit me.'
>
> "Then the righteous will answer him, 'Lord, when did we see you hungry and feed you, or thirsty and give you something to drink? When did we see you a stranger and invite you in, or needing clothes and clothe you? When did we see you sick or in prison and go to visit you?'
>
> "The King will reply, 'Truly I tell you, whatever you did for one of the least of these brothers and sisters of mine, you did for me.'

"Then he will say to those on his left, 'Depart from me, you who are cursed, into the eternal fire prepared for the devil and his angels. For I was hungry and you gave me nothing to eat, I was thirsty and you gave me nothing to drink, I was a stranger and you did not invite me in, I needed clothes and you did not clothe me, I was sick and in prison and you did not look after me.'

"They also will answer, 'Lord, when did we see you hungry or thirsty or a stranger or needing clothes or sick or in prison, and did not help you?'

"He will reply, 'Truly I tell you, whatever you did not do for one of the least of these, you did not do for me.'

"Then they will go away to eternal punishment, but the righteous to eternal life." (Matthew 25:31-46)

In this Bible passage, Jesus tells us that God notices how we treat other people, especially those who are His elect. God loves His people. If we are kind to them, then we are kind to Him. If we are indifferent and uncaring toward God's people, then we are indifferent and uncaring toward God. We should always be generous to our brothers and sisters in Christ, remembering that God loves them and that He counts kindness toward them as kindness toward Himself.

CONCLUSION

Look up Romans 12:13 in your Bible and copy it here:

REMEMBER! Be hospitable to all God's people.

> ## PART 2: MR. WEAK AND MR. HALTING
> ### READ PAGES 222–225.

DO YOU REMEMBER?

The pilgrims were _____ , and so they went to the home

of _____ . He received them kindly and gave them _____ .

The next day, Gaius asked them to help him kill _____ ,

the robber who was holding a captive. _____ fought

Slaygood and killed him, freeing Mr. _____ .

CHARACTERS

What do these characters' names mean?

Mr. Weak _____

Mr. Halting _____

Notright _____

Answer the questions below:

1. How had Mr. Weak managed to get up Difficult Hill?

    _____

2. Did Mr. Notright try to help Mr. Weak escape from the robbers?

    _____

3. What happened to Mr. Notright after he ran away from Slaygood?

    _____

4. Who married Mercy? _____

5. Who traveled with Mr. Weak as the pilgrims went on?

    _____

SYMBOLISM

In this portion of *Pilgrim's Progress*, John Bunyan emphasizes God's care for those who are ill or disabled. Mr. Weak is unable to travel quickly.

He has often been left behind by other pilgrims. However, when Notright runs away and leaves Mr. Weak to the robbers, God is clearly angry. His judgment falls on Notright.

    The good pilgrims assure Mr. Weak that they will help him, even if it means they must travel more slowly. They also permit Mr. Halting to join them. Mr. Halting is a particular encouragement to Mr. Weak. Often, people who have similar struggles can empathize with each other and help each other. Mr. Halting may seem like a burden to other people, but to Mr. Weak, he is a great blessing, and they travel well together.

BIBLE READING

    When Mr. Weak worries that he will be a burden to his fellow pilgrims, Greatheart responds by quoting a verse in I Thessalonians:

> And we urge you, brothers and sisters, warn those who are idle and disruptive, encourage the disheartened, help the weak, be patient with everyone. (I Thessalonians 5:14)

    God instructs us to warn those who are inclined to sin (those who are idle and disruptive), but also to be patient with everyone, especially those who are weak. In God's providence, there are many people who have severe struggles. Perhaps they have had terrible experiences in life or maybe they have a physical or mental handicap. We should be gentle with these people, encouraging and helping them in Christian faith.

CONCLUSION

Read the story below and answer the questions.

Brenda went to Sunday school class one morning to find a new student sitting at the table. The new boy was a little funny-looking. She smiled at him, but he did not look at her. He twisted his fingers and hummed to himself. Brenda thought he was odd.

"Good morning class," said the Sunday school teacher. "We have a new student this morning. His name is Bobby."

"Bobby," said Bobby. That was all he said.

"Bobby has autism," the teacher told the class. "He can't talk very well, and he doesn't always understand what we say. But I am sure you will all help him and make him feel welcome."

The class felt a little uncomfortable with Bobby there. He just sat and twisted his fingers together when the teacher asked the class questions. He did not open his Bible to read with everyone else. During craft time, when the class cut and glued some pictures, the teacher had to help Bobby with the scissors. Bobby slowed everyone down.

Brenda's friend Sara leaned over and whispered, "I don't like having Bobby in our class. He is funny-looking, and he can't even use scissors. Maybe if we make fun of him, he won't come back anymore."

How should Brenda respond to her friend Sara?

_____

_____

_____

In our last lesson, we learned that God wants us to be kind and hospitable to other people. Does this include people like Bobby?

_____

 REMEMBER!   Be patient with everyone, especially those who are weak or disabled.

> ## PART 3: THE HOME OF MNASON
> ### READ PAGES 225-229.

DO YOU REMEMBER?

Mr. _____ told the pilgrims that _____

had run away and left him when they were attacked by _____.

Mr. Weak worried that he traveled too _____ for the other

pilgrims, but they assured him he was _____.

As they traveled, they met Mr. _____ , who joined

them and became a good _____ to Mr. Weak.

CHARACTERS

What do these characters' names mean?

Mr. Contrite: _____

Mr. Holy: _____

Mr. Lovesaint: _____

Mr. Truthful: _____

Mr. Penitent: _____

Answer the questions below:

1. When Christiana and her friends arrived in the town of Vanity, where did they stay?

   _____

2. How had Faithful's death affected the attitude of the town toward Christians?

   _____

3. Who visited the pilgrims at Mnason's home?

   _____

4. Whom did Samuel and Joseph marry? _____

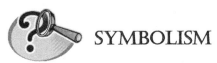

SYMBOLISM

Christiana and her friends do not encounter the same difficulties that Christian and Faithful faced in the town of Vanity. The murder of Faithful has made the town feel guilty. They have not truly repented, but they do have enough sense of their own wrongdoing to prevent them from terrorizing Christians anymore.

Mr. Honesty notes that some events may have unexpected outcomes. No one would have anticipated that Faithful's death would make things better for other Christians in the town, and yet it did.

God can turn even terrible sins to good purposes. He can take a bad thing and use it to accomplish something wonderful. If we trust Him, then we see after a while that He is working for the good of His people.

BIBLE READING

The Bible tells us that God makes things beautiful, even when we do not understand His work:

> He has made everything beautiful in its time. He has also set eternity in the human heart; yet no one can fathom what God has done from beginning to end. (Ecclesiastes 3:11)

Sometimes, we have terrible experiences or go through great temptations and trials, but God is with us. No one can understand everything God does, but we can trust Him. We know that, in time, He works everything for the good of those who love Him (Romans 8:8).

CONCLUSION

Can you think of a story in the Bible about a terrible thing that God used for a good purpose? Write it below:

_____

_____

_____

 REMEMBER! God makes everything beautiful in its time.

CHAPTER 18: CHRISTIANA AT THE DELECTABLE MOUNTAINS

PART 1: GIANT DESPAIR
READ PAGES 230-233.

DO YOU REMEMBER?

Christiana, Mercy, and the other pilgrims finally arrived in the town of

_____ , and they stayed at the home of Mnason. Contrite told

them that the town had been safer since the death of _____.

During their stay in Vanity, Samuel married _____,

and Joseph married _____ .

CHARACTERS

What do these characters' names mean?

Despondency: _____

Fearful: _____

Answer the questions below:

1. Whose castle did Christiana and her friends encounter on the way to the Delectable Mountains?

    _____

2. What did Greatheart think they should do?

    _____

3. What was the name of Giant Despair's club? _____

4. After Greatheart and his friends killed Giant Despair, who did they find imprisoned in the castle?

    _____

 SYMBOLISM

In his story about Greatheart at Doubting Castle, John Bunyan continues his theme regarding the necessity of Christians helping each other. Greatheart is not a victim of Giant Despair, yet he decides to go out and fight him. Greatheart remembers that everything rightfully belongs to God. Instead of hanging back in safer places, he ventures out on the attack, claiming back the land for Christ.

Like Greatheart, we should remember that all things rightfully belong to God. There is no place where sin should be permitted to dwell. We should spread the good news of Jesus wherever we can. When we do so, we may help some people who are held captive in sin. God may use us to free them and set them on the right path.

BIBLE READING

King David wrote a psalm about victory over enemies:

> Praise be to the LORD my Rock,
> who trains my hands for war,
> my fingers for battle.
> He is my loving God and my fortress,
> my stronghold and my deliverer,
> my shield, in whom I take refuge,
> who subdues peoples under me.
>
> (Psalm 144:1-2)

In Christian life, our enemies are sin and Satan. God trains us to fight those things. We fight them in our own lives every day, as we learn to obey God and to resist temptation. Sometimes, we can even help others in their battles, like Greatheart helped Despondency and Fearful.

We can help others by praying for them, being kind to them, and reminding them of God's promises and warnings. The Word of God is our sword in battle against sin and Satan. When we help others remember the Scriptures, we support them in the fight. However, we must do this gently, with patience for those who are weak and struggling.

CONCLUSION

Sometimes, people are trapped in despair, just like Despondency and Fearful in our story. They need someone to help them. Suppose your friend says to you, "I am very sad. I want to be a Christian and obey God, but I don't know whether God loves me at all."

What can you say to remind your friend of the promises in God's Word?

_____

_____

 REMEMBER! When others are discouraged, it is good to remind them of the promises in God's Word.

PART 2: MR. VALIANT-FOR-TRUTH
READ PAGES 233-237.

DO YOU REMEMBER?

When the pilgrims came to _____ Castle, Greatheart told

them that they should go fight Giant _____ . The giant took his

club called _____ and fought, but Greatheart and the others

_____ him. Inside the castle, they found _____

and his daughter Fearful and set them _____.

CHARACTERS
What do these characters' names mean?

Envy _____

Illwill _____

Valiant-for-Truth _____

Wildhead _____

Inconsiderate_____

Pragmatic _____

Answer the questions below:

1. How did Greatheart recognize the Lord's true shepherds?

    _____

2. What was Despondency's dream? _____

    _____

3. What happened when Envy and Illwill threw mud at Mr. Godly?

    _____

4. According to the shepherd, why did the tailor not run out of cloth?

    _____

    _____

5. Who attacked Valiant-for-Truth? _____

_____

6. How long did Valiant-for-Truth fight? _____

 SYMBOLISM

The shepherds show the pilgrims several lessons about rewards for obedience to God. In the first lesson, Envy and Illwill throw mud at Mr. Godly, but the mud slips off without any effect. There are many times that people who are jealous or disruptive will try to stir up trouble against a righteous person. However, the righteous do not even need to bother about trying to brush off the silly accusations and gossip. If they simply continue to do right, then the people attacking them will begin to look foolish in the eyes of others.

In the second lesson, the tailor makes clothes for the poor, but his cloth does not run out. When we are generous, God rewards us. Certainly, we should be wise steward of the good things God has given us, but we should also not be stingy. When we share, we often discover that we have more than we need.

The third lesson shows people trying to wash the darkness off a dark-skinned person. John

Bunyan uses this picture to illustrate that only God can cleanse a sinner. We cannot change the heart of a sinner any more than we can change someone's skin color by washing it. The other part of this lesson, however, is that we do not know the nature of someone's heart by looking at the outside. The dark-skinned person may be the most righteous person before God, and the light-skinned people may be the most evil on the inside. We should never judge someone by their skin color, hair color, or anything else on the outside. Only God knows what is in a person's heart.

As the travelers leave the Delectable Mountains, they encounter Valiant-for-Truth. He has been attacked, but he has fought bravely. The battle of Valiant-for-Truth emphasizes that we must cling tightly to the truth of God. Sometimes we may be tempted to turn aside because another way is easier. People may tell us that our faith is outdated or impractical. But we should listen only to God's Word. God is true, and those who love the truth love Him.

 ## BIBLE READING

Psalm 15 tells us that God is pleased with those who speak the truth:

> LORD, who may dwell in your sacred tent?
> Who may live on your holy mountain?
> The one whose walk is blameless,
> who does what is righteous,
> who speaks the truth from their heart.
>
> (Psalm 15:1-2)

God is true, and when we honor the truth, we honor God. Obviously, we should not lie to others. We should also speak the truth in our own hearts. Sometimes people lie to themselves. They pretend that they are not sinning, even when they are. We must honor truth in *every* aspect of life—believing the Scriptures, speaking the truth, and acknowledging the truth in our own hearts, even if it means admitting when we are wrong about something.

CONCLUSION

Find John 4:24 in your Bible and copy it below:

_____

_____

_____

 REMEMBER! Love the truth!

CHAPTER 19: ON THE ENCHANTED GROUND

READ PAGES 238-245.

DO YOU REMEMBER?

The _____ showed the pilgrims some lessons at the

_____ Mountains. First, they saw two men flinging

_____ at Mr. Godly, but it did not stick to him. Second, they saw

a _____ making clothes for the poor. Finally, they saw several

people trying to change a man's heart by _____ him. Later,

they met Valiant-for-_____ , who had fought bravely.

CHARACTERS
What do these characters' names mean?

Heedless: _____

Self-Confidence: _____

Standfast: _____

Answer the questions below:

1. What were Heedless and Self-Confidence doing on the Enchanted Ground?

    _____

2. What happened when Greatheart shook Heedless and Self-Confidence?

    _____

3. What was Standfast doing on the Enchanted Ground?

    _____

4. Who tempted Standfast with money and fame?

    _____

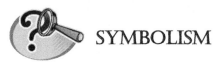 SYMBOLISM

The Enchanted Ground symbolizes laziness which may descend upon believers when Christian life becomes routine. Sometimes people may stop praying or reading the Scriptures. They may become **heedless** (paying no attention to danger) or they may trust in themselves rather than in God (**self-confidence**). John Bunyan warns that we must remain alert, even when life feels comfortable. It is too easy to gradually slip away from our duties before God. We have to pay attention.

Standfast was praying when the other pilgrims discovered him. Prayer is an excellent means of remaining spiritually alert. When we feel tempted to stop attending church or drift away from the Scriptures, we should pray and ask God for strength.

Standfast was particularly tempted by Madam Bubble. A **bubble** is shiny and pretty, but it has no substance. If you try to hold it, the bubble vanishes. Madam Bubble symbolizes this fake attraction. She is pretty. She freely offers Standfast wealth and fame. However, if Standfast had gone with her, he would have found her promises all empty. She would have dragged him to hell.

John Bunyan warns of things that appear attractive on the outside. We must evaluate them carefully according to God's Word. We should be cautious, not allowing ourselves to run after everything that looks good. Some things may appear to offer great benefits, but the end is destruction.

BIBLE READING

The psalms contain many beautiful prayers. Sometimes, when we are tempted to be lazy in our Christian faith, we do not feel like praying. At times like that, it is good to remember the prayers of the psalms. If we cannot think of anything else, we can always pray those prayers. The psalms remind us to bring everything to God in prayer.

Listen to my words, LORD,
consider my lament.
Hear my cry for help,
my King and my God,
for to you I pray.
In the morning, LORD, you hear my voice;
in the morning I lay my requests before you
and wait expectantly.

(Psalm 5:1-3)

Especially when we are tempted, we must cry out to God. He hears our prayers and strengthens us against temptation.

CONCLUSION

Can you find another prayer in Psalms? You will not have to look very hard. The book of Psalms is full of prayers!

Write the references of two more prayers in the book of Psalms:

_____

_____

 REMEMBER! Pray every day, even when you do not feel like praying. God will strengthen you.

CHAPTER 20: BEULAH LAND

READ PAGES 246–256.

DO YOU REMEMBER?

The pilgrims found two men sleeping on the _____

Ground. They tried to _____ them, but the men only muttered

in their sleep. Later, they found _____ praying. Standfast

told them that he had been tempted by Madame _____ .

Answer the questions below:

1. Who was the first pilgrim from Christiana's group to cross the river?

    _____

2. Why did Mr. Halting give away his crutches when he received the summons to the Celestial City?

    _____

3. What were Mr. Honesty's last words?

_____

4. In the story, which of the pilgrims crossed the river last?

_____

5. Where did the pilgrims go after they crossed the river?

_____

SYMBOLISM

The river symbolizes death. Each of the pilgrims in turn is called to cross it. Several of them mention that they have been afraid of crossing the river, because nearly everyone has sometimes feared death. However, when faced with the river, they realize that they are ready after all. Even Despondency and Fearful cross over confidently. God gives grace to His people to face death. They do not need to be afraid. He helps and supports them as they pass from this life into glory.

Each of the pilgrims talks to the others, and some of them leave gifts. Valiant-for-Truth leaves his sword, and Mr. Halting leaves his crutch. These are tokens of remembrance to help those who are still struggling through life. When we remember the strength of those who have gone before us, we are encouraged in our faith. We remember the courage of people who fought for truth, and we remember the perseverance of people who trusted in God. These things comfort us and remind us of the hope of heaven.

In heaven, all things are made new. Mr. Halting could leave his crutch behind, knowing that he would not need it anymore. Despondency and Fearful know they will be delivered from oppressing fears. Even in the sadness of death, we can rejoice. Those who put their faith in Christ are delivered from suffering as they pass through the river of death.

BIBLE READING

Job was a man who suffered much in life. The Bible tells us that he had once been very rich, but he lost everything, including his own children. Job had many reasons to be discouraged, but he made one of the most wonderful statements of faith recorded in the Scriptures:

I know that my redeemer lives,
and that in the end he will stand on the earth.
And after my skin has been destroyed,
yet in my flesh I will see God;
I myself will see him
with my own eyes—I, and not another.
How my heart yearns within me!

(Job 19:25-27)

Even amid great trials, God strengthened Job. Job was able to remember the promises of God. He knew that someday after he died, he would see God, and he yearned for that wonderful day.

This is our hope also. Even though life is difficult, and even though death is sad, we know that our Redeemer lives. Someday, we will see Him face to face.

CONCLUSION

Find John 11:25-26 in the Bible. Copy it here:

_____

_____

_____

_____

 REMEMBER! Our Redeemer lives!

Made in the USA
Coppell, TX
28 May 2020

26596258R00077